MY FIRST BOOK OF POEMS

Johnny Lee Stillwagner

ISBN 979-8-89243-690-8 (paperback)
ISBN 979-8-89130-600-4 (digital)

Christian Faith Publishing
832 Park Avenue
Meadville, PA 16335
www.christianfaithpublishing.com

Printed in the United States of America

Contents

An Everlasting Love...
Faded Away

Wheat has left the fields
Sky is turning gray
She will never know how I felt
      For now she has passed away.

    LATE SIXTIES, WE BECAME FRIENDS
    SEVENTIES, LOVERS, EXPERIENCING PAIN
    EIGHTIES, PARENTS, LONERS, HOPING
      TO CROSS PATHS AGAIN

A distant Shadow, Time is ever so clear
A World of Lost and Lonely
Coming hither, Going there
We Seek Refuge, in Greed and Lust
One day we will Learn
    it all turns to Dust

    Memories—Rhetoric and Sublime
    Moments of pleasure, fortune, and Thyme
    Truth held so Steadfast and True
    Lies and deceit; broken into

Children Treasured, Hers and Mine
Children treasured, making a bind
Life Shared, Love Lost
    Yesterday a Blessing—Today is Lost!

    In Memoriam
    JOHNNY LEE STILLWAGNER
    DEC. 16, 1993

A Reflection of Life

Look through any window, Tell me what do you see?
Is it a reflection…of who you are, or what you wish to be.
Are the wrinkles on your face; a sign of old age or the
      experience of life.
Have you received praise and respect from your peers,
     or just an acknowledge "How do" from a passerby.

Block a part of your reflection.
Does it change your person, or can you see a
     different personality!

Can your life reflect your image.
Was it panoramic or just enough to get by?
Are you the picture of what you
     wanted to be,
Or an image of someone…you wished to be.

A reflection on life; a few seconds
     to change or a lifetime of changes.

December 31, 1994

You Were Born to Live

Let Faith Be The Key
    When you walk in Life's Miseries.
Let Love Be Your Guide,
    When Hell's Darkness Blankets Your Eyes.

For You're The Reason…
You Were Born To Live!

When You Doubt Your Capabilities
    and Life doesn't seem worth Living…
When all your problems
    seem to stack in bundles
Then it's Time
    for you to join the gig

We Weren't meant to be frightened
We're not here for fightin'
We're here to experience Love
And Live For God Above

The Hell of Life
The Hopes of Love
All you've ever wanted
seems to wash out in a flood
It all seems so unreal
It all climbs downhill

If you really want to enjoy…
let Faith Be The Key
    When You Walk In Life's Miseries.

Let Love Be Your Guide,
    When Hell's Darkness Blankets Your Eyes.
For You're The Reason
You Were Born To Live!

Time

A Man once said,
    "There never seems to be
        enough Time, to do the
Things you wish to do"

But I Say,
    "There is a Time,
        and Season,
    For everything
        under the Sun,"

And with God on your side,
    "We only have
        Just Begun"

I Love You

To Catherine May, I Love You

Tell me you love me baby,
    Tell me you are mine.

For each time we're apart
    You are constantly in my heart.

Like a bird in flight
    Aware of thy destination.
I think of you day and night.

For you're the center
    Of all observation.

If a tree becomes uprooted
    We replace it twofold.
So its roots
    Withstand all durability
And is stable in the wind.

My heart loves you.
    If you be in doubt,
    I'll come to you
Like a bird in flight
    Flying in concourse
        Through the night.

I'll relinquish your doubts
    And fears,

But to replace your faith,
    To uproot what misconceptions
        You may conceive,

I must first
    Search my soul.

For honesty
    Must be born,

After what we believe
    Was torn,

Through not trusting
    In the love
        We had

        For each other!

How High's the Water

To live life
In the face of reality
　　Can be an illusion.

Circumstances may seem
　　Periodical to an
　　　　Exercise of agility.

But!
　　An extended hand
　　　　From one
Provides a security
　　A thirteen-year-old understands
An inescapable journey
　　overcome
assures the assessment
　　of
　　　　life
　　　　　　hereafter.

Run, Kelly, Run

5'6" IS PRETTY
         FAR
FOR A BROAD JUMP…
         JUMP
RUN, KELLY, RUN
IF THIS WAS A SONG
       BEING SUNG
THERE WOULD BE
DRAMATIC TEMPO
AND A MELANCHOLY RHYTHM
      OF DRUMS
THE BAND WOULD PLAY ON AND ON…

BUT AS YOU,
    AM I
ONLY AVERAGE
     WITH SIMPLE SIGHTS
BUT RUN ON
BABY,
RUN STRONG.

MAYBE TOMORROW,
YOUR SONG
     WILL BE SUNG!

In Memoriam
(To My Grandparents)

Someone Dear To Me,
    Passed Away Today.
Yet I Don't Recall
    How He Looked
        Or The Time Of Day.
But What I've Mentioned
    Has Little Importance.

It's What He Did,
    And Who He Was,
        That Makes Me Remember.

Many Miss Him
Some Always Will.

I Pray,
    That Eternity Be His.

And For Us Remaining
God's Love
    And Goodwill!

May he rest in peace!

You're His Mother, and He Is Your Son

(I'm His Mother And He's My Son)
HE IS NO LONGER YOUNG,
    AS YOU MAY EXPECT HIM TO BE
(I'm Much Older Than I Care To Admit)
HE'S SPENT SOME TIME AT SEA
    AS WELL AS MANY COUNTRIES
(I've Got The Wrinkles To Prove It)
HE CLAIMS TO BE THE SAME
(No He Is No Longer The Same)
HE'LL BE COMING HOME SOON
(I'll Treat Him Different
    With More Respect)
DON'T WORRY
    OR BE AFRAID
(I Love Him
    With All My Heart)
AND HE LOVES YOU
    IN A SON'S MOST SPECIAL WAY!

Buried Grandfather

UNITED STATES
NAVAL AVIATION WEAPONS FACILITY
FPO NEW YORK 09515

IN REPLY REFER TO:

THEY
　　BURIED
　　　　MY
　　　　　　GRANDFATHER
　　　　　　　TODAY.

TODAY
　　I
　　　　DIDN'T
　　　　　　EAT.
　　　　　　　DIDN'T
　　　　　　　　　SLEEP.

TODAY
　　I'LL KNOW
HE'S ON THE RIGHT HAND
　　OF THE THRONE.

TOMORROW,
　　I'LL
　　　　MOURN
　　　　　　BECAUSE
　　　　　I'LL
　　　　　　　MISS
　　　　　　　　HIM.

I'M HERE
AND HE'S THERE
MY GRANDFATHER
HAS TAUGHT ME
    TO RELIEVE MY FEARS.

THOUGH OTHERS HAVE LEFT
THEY LIVED AND DID THEIR BEST,
BUT CLARENCE
    WAS SPECIAL
AND HE MEANT A LOT TO ME.

Two of Us

UNITED STATES
NAVAL AVIATION WEAPONS FACILITY
FPO NEW YORK 09515

IN REPLY REFER TO:

THE TWO OF US
    WERE AS ONE.
WORKING, LAUGHING,
    BEING TOGETHER.

NOW I'M ONE

THE SUN ISN'T SHINING TODAY
NOR, I DOUBT, IF IT WILL.

I'M ALONE AND LONELY
AND NOW
    I ALWAYS WILL.

"REST IN PEACE"

Jill Marie (One)

A BLACK CAT;
A BROKEN GLASS
    ONCE REFLECTED
        WHEN GAZED UPON…
A BIRTH

WHEN ONE HOPES
WHEN ONE DREAMS
WHEN ONE GESTURES…
(FOR SAFETY OF LIFE)

THEN CAN I REJOICE
WHEN GIVEN A JOY

SUCH
    AS
        YOU
            HAVE
GIVEN ME!

THANK YOU

Jill Marie (Two)

Soon again
    To be together
Two, (of us)
Three (of ours)
Forever

Then I can honestly say,
The birth of a child
Is greater
    Than answering
        The call of the wild!

For together
    Living is wilder
        Than I
            Could ever experience

Alone

Jill Marie (Three)

When (she) was delivered
Were (you) blinded
    By her beauty,

Did you gasp
When the doc
    Smacked her ass!

Were you depressed
    Because I wasn't there?

Did you cry?
    When you saw
        Her smile?

Did you think of me?
    When she fell asleep!

I was hoping for you, and still do!
I think I was nervous, and still am!

Jill Marie (Four)

My twenty-third tear
    has come and gone
and to expect
    much more
      than you've
        already given

is useless
    unless you
      could give
      me
        you
          tonight!

then I'd have everything!

My Girl

Sometimes it's hard to know
     what your heart is feeling
And harder still to put into words

Love is Simple… You can't define it
It's not the words but the thought
     behind it that counts.

My Girl
Well she's everything a love could possibly be
My Girl
Makes Love the way I always dreamed it would be

Deep down inside I know
What I should be saying
But every time I try it comes out wrong

I'm glad our Love is a Love forever
And when we're alone together
She knows me, She shows me

My Girl
Well she's everything a love could possibly be
My Girl
Makes Love the way I always dreamed it would be

I'd need a lifetime
To show her all the Love I have to give
and hold her in my heart
for as long as I Live

We'll stick together
Like the Moon and the Nighttime
Happy forever

I could spend my Lifetime
So in Love With
My Girl

Cat—I Love You

Couldn't Be
  A Man
  Without Your Love,
  Without Your Touch,
  Without
    A Part Of Life
That You Are To Me.

After
  Twenty-Three Lonely Years
  You Answered, "I DO"
    With Full Knowledge and Understanding
Of What I Expected Of You.

Today
  We Live Our Lives
  In Understanding and Intimacy
  Giving and Sharing
  Caring For Our Children
    And Appreciating
      All We Mean
        To One Another.

In That Aspect

Love is
Ours in a
Very Meaningful Relationship
Enjoyed To The Fullest Extent

You Are The Love
Of My Life, With That
Understanding… Do You Want To Make Love, Fool Around
Get Under The Covers, Get It On, Do It
Get Naked… Tell Me You Need Me,
Even If It's A Lie!

"The Love of My Life"

Hold Me Baby
    Get Close To Me
Do Me Baby
    Show Me
        That You Love Me

All That I Am
All That I Do Girl
    Not For The Love
        Of The World
All For The Love
    Of You Girl

    You're The Rarest Of Jewels
    More Precious Than Gold
    You're The Very Center Of My Soul

    You're As Sweet As Wine
    You Taste So Divine

You're the Love
    Of
        My
            Life.

Times of Happiness

To Remember The Memories
      Some Good, Others Sad.
With Girls, Or Parents,
      Or The Many Friends I've Had.

Now Because Of The Military Restraints
      On My Life,
These Memories are now more
      Sensitive and Remembered.

I Realize I Can't Live On Those Memories,
      As I Can't Live On Last Week's Meal.
But Their Perseverance Is Like A Jam,
      Stored But Never Forgotten
      Later Bringing Spice… Loving In Years.

Now These Memories Are Being
      Remembered Again
As In The Future,
      Will Be
            Times Of Happiness

Because Of Them.

Cat

The Look In Your Eyes
First Green… Then Blue
You See Me… As No One Could

The Touch of Your Embrace
The Expression on Your Face
You Let Me Know
I Make You Feel Good…

When We're Apart
A Know No One Takes My Place

The Day May Be Long… From Dusk to Dawn
But You're The Most Faithful
Best Friend A Man Could Have

Cat
Never Have I Known… A Person Quite Like You
You Only Complain… When The Worse Experience
Never Lets Up
But You Always Know The Right Words
To Cheer Me Up

You're
everything
a
man
dreams
of

You're Catherine May
And You're MY Woman
And You Belong To Me
JOHNNY LEE

I Never Sleep

When you want me
    I'll be there.
When you need me.
    I'll be anywhere.

Ask me,
    "Please"

I need you
As you need me,

That's what life is all about,
    To be there.

I can sleep
    Elsewhere.

May 11, 1976

Hey, Close Your Eyes

Hey,
Close your eyes.
Think of the sun.
Let the rain come.

Turn off the lights,
Turn them on!
There's always the silence
Even after the storm!

Think of a song,
Sing-a-long.
For the only solution to reality
Is time!

And it's christmastime again.

Have a good one!

December 9, 1979

My Grandfather

My grandfather
        is not a rich old man,
but he makes a lot of sense
        to me.
And he did his share
        in the family plan.

Now they're all grown up,
        a few have passed away.
But Grandfather is still around.
He's agile, talented, and pretty smart.
I'll always remember him that way.

Recently pneumonia has struck,
        but even that hasn't got him down
        completely
why if I know him
        he's pinched the nurse
        and even tugged on her gown.

Most likely not,
        for he's eighty-three,
                and one hell of a man.

I guess what I'm trying to say.
is I'm proud to be his grandson.

And I'll be coming home soon,
and what I'll be expecting to see,
is my grandfather sitting on his porch,
looking up the road, and waiting on me!

He's Eighty-Three

MANY YEARS COUNTED
    COME AND GONE.
NOW HE'S DOWN
UNABLE TO STAND HIS GROUND.

I'M HERE
    AND HE'S THERE
MY GRANDFATHER,
    HAS TAUGHT ME
    TO RELIEVE MY FEARS.

A COAL MINER (THIRTY-EIGHT YEARS)
    FEW MEN COULD BE FINER
    BUT NOW HAS SLOWED SOME.
PNEUMONIA HAS SEEPED IN
BUT HIS TEMPERAMENT
    HAS REMAINED UNCREASED.
HE IS TOUCHED
AND UNABLE TO FIGHT IT
    'CAUSE HE'S EIGHTY-SOME
    AND HIS TIME HAS COME.

HIS WORK THROUGH THE AGES
    SEEMS COUNTLESS
THOUGH HIS BODY
    PROVES THE MARKS
HIS MIND IS STILL SOUND.
HIS FAMILY AND FRIENDS,
    THEY'LL ALL REMEMBER HIM.

Lovely Weekend

ANOTHER LONG,
    LONELY
        WEEKEND!
COMES TO AN END.
    I WILL THINK OF YOU,
        BEFORE
            I
                SLEEP.
AND THINK OF YOU AGAIN
        WHEN
            I
                WAKE
AND HOPE
        YOU
            THINK
                OF
                    ME
                        OFTEN.

SEPTEMBER 1978
SCOTLAND

The Last I Saw of Him

UNITED STATES
NAVAL AVIATION WEAPONS FACILITY
FPO NEW YORK 09515

IN REPLY REFER TO:

THE LAST I SAW OF HIM,
IS THE WAY I SHALL REMEMBER HIM.
FOR NOT IN PAIN
NOR IN NEED
JUST A SIMPLE MAN
ANSWERING TO MY HEED.

GIVING ALL THAT I ASKED.

ADVISE FOR A GARDEN,
AND NEXT YEAR'S SOLUTIONS
TO LAST YEAR'S PROBLEMS.

WHEN I LAST SAW HIM
I WISHED
I COULD
HAVE TOLD HIM,

I LOVE YOU.

BUT,
HE
ALREADY
KNEW
THAT.

Going Home

The Wood-Burning Train
    Comes Slowly Down The Track
Many Southern Men
    Stand Solemnly, Attentive,
       And Somber
And Pay Their Last Respects
    To A Legend.

One They Could Find Little Fault
One Who Lived A Life
    They Only Dreamed
       They Could Have Lived.
One Who To Many Was An Outlaw

But To Them
    A Victim Of Circumstances

And To Die A Death
    From One Who Was Treated As A Guest
       Fed And Refreshed,

Then Turned Traitor
    To Be Remembered
       As The Man
Who Shot Jesse James

I Now Understand

to my father

I now understand, somewhat,
    of the decision you had to face.
Other times, I don't seem to
    understand at all.

The hell of life, love, hopes.
I see what you wish for each of
    us to be.

Your decision played an important
    part of my life, you know.

I wish now
    that then I would have awakened.

I guess I'm doing that now.

February 20, 1976

All My Love, Your Son

Through my writings I share
The love of life, hopes,
    Sometimes hard to bear
Though a letter
Shares one's lifestyle
A poem/song
Relates more feeling
    To those you want to know and share

Many years have passed
Since I was your young son
But a son I shall always be
Sometimes far away
But in a mother's heart
    Always near

More years shall slip on by
And each of us
    Will get older

When I write (what may seem like never),
Remember
In the future
I'll be there forever
All my love,
Your son

To Mrs. Wilson

WE LOVE YOU
YOUR FACE
    NOW SOMEWHAT SWOLLEN,
BUT
    YOUR HEART
    REMAINS GOLDEN.

WHILE YOUR SIDE
    HAS A SLIGHT LOSS OF AGILITY,
YOUR PEACE OF MIND
    REMAINS
        WITH YOUR WONDERFUL CONTROL
          OF STABILITY.

WE LOVE YOU,
    FOR WHAT YOU ARE.
WE LOVE YOU,
    AS WE LOVE THE STARS.

REMAIN WITH US
GUIDE US
SHARE WITH US
    THIS BEAUTIFUL HOLIDAY SEASON.

I Saw a Girl Tonight

I Was In The Club
God How She Reminds Me So,
    Of A Face
       I Once Knew,
A Long Time Ago,
    In The Candlelight.
It Seems This Place
    Is Giving Me Punishment Undo.

"When Will I See You Again"
    Just Came On.
God,
    Even The Jukebox Is Cold.
Oh Well,
    It Makes Me Respect Home.

ODE to a Sailor's Mother

How long has it been,
    since your youngest son has been home?
(two years)
Have you missed his love,
    his time away from home?
(very much)
When was the last time
    you saw his face?
(I can't remember)
When was the last time
    you and he embraced?
(Much too long)

Was your son as handsome
    as he was before?
(much, much more)
Is he as clever and witty
    as the Jones' boy next door?
(ten times... if not more)
Do you remember the love
    you felt for him?
Are you still proud
    as you've always been?
(as much as a mother could)

You asked for a poem.
    one with only you in mind.
So this I write to you
    truly making it
        one of a kind.

Heart, mind, liberty, and love
    could hardly be written
        on short space as such.

But I will speak to you
on what I think of much

Think of god,
    Micky,
        and the rest you wish to speak.

If laughter,
    a smile,
        and tears appear

A fact of life,
    has been proven.
to have
    life,
        and
            friendship

is to have love.

Always a friend,
Love, John

October 10, 1976

Mother

The River Is Wide
      The Mountains Are High
            Too Steep To Cross In A Day

You're A Beauty
      As Well As Sweet
And You Have An Endless
      Sacrificing Love

I, Your Son,
      Am Restless And Young
            But You Have Always Known This

To Tell You All I Think Of You
Is As The River And Mountain

Too Much To Say
In A Single Day

Elvis

ELVIS
You have left…what few could give
You have upset…those who thought you were dear

Once you've confessed your Love…
    You gave all you had to give.
If circumstances weren't right
    You tried to make them right.

ELVIS… His Presence Meant A Lot To Me
    Now He's Gone… His Memory So Clear.
ELVIS… Gentle, Fun-Loving, And Polite
ELVIS… Was The God-Fearing Kind.

When Appearing… You Rocked and You Rolled
You Twisted, You Shouted
You Made The Public Squirm With Delight
You Spoke of a Greater Being… You Sang It With Love
You Reached Out To Others
    Some… who would have robbed you blind

You are Forever
    To Us Who Thought You Were Dear
With All You Had

You Left What Few Could Give…

You Left Us Your Presence

Song (Elvis Was Love)

He lives in the splendor of heaven
He knew of his destiny
He left with millions mourning
    Yes, Elvis meant a lot to me.
    Elvis was love
    and he had a gift from above
    Elvis knew and accepted a life
    where others would never have tried.

He wrote of many salvations
He cried for many lost souls
He tried with a strong determination
and now he has reached his goal.
    Elvis was love
    and he had a gift from above
    Elvis knew and accepted a life
    Where others would never have tried.
Even now
    time has passed much too quickly
As a man of music I mourn
    but I know that all must depart sometime
I just wish Elvis would
    never have gone.

    Elvis was love
    and he had a gift from above
    Elvis knew and accepted a life
    where others would never have tried.

Ooh Elvis—hear me calling
    Speak, so others will find.
      "Elvis was love"

To an Old Man I Met in Singapore

He's just an old man
    aged in years
living a long life
    with long-lost tears

Much knowledge has seeped through his mind
    not of intellect and statistics
but common-sense wise

He has loved many
    and loved by much
but years bring forgetting
    especially with our world as such.

A shame the young live
    life with trips of their own
Never learning what can give
    from an old man's bones

So to the man of old
    I will receive the tears you once knew
and of the knowledge you told

It's much sad for me
    the things you saw I will see
If I just listen while I live
    I know what's to be

About the Author

Born in 1955, in Phoenix, Arizona, a retired United States Navy Veteran, Johnny resides in Wayne County, Ohio, with his wife, Nancy, and two cats: Callie and Snookie.